Helping Children See Jesus

LIVING FAITH

A Family Worship Study on the Letter from James

Illustrator: James Nguyen   Page Layout: Lindsay Hess
Author: Jeffrey Kilcup
Hymn Typeset Credit: Grace Music; Bible Visuals International

© 2023 Bible Visuals International
PO Box 153, Akron, PA 17501-0153
Phone: (717) 859-1131
www.biblevisuals.org
ISBN 978-1-64104-261-1

Special thanks to Josh Scherrer for providing editorial feedback for this volume. Thanks to Grace Music for graciously providing many of the typeset hymns.

BVI is a 501(c)(3) charity organization. We rely on the support of ministry partners like you to help us in our mission of Helping Children See Jesus. If you would like to learn more, please visit biblevisuals.org.

What can my family learn through this Bible study?

Your family will be encouraged to read God's Word together and worship Him in the beauty of His holiness

You will understand the themes and outline of an entire book of the Bible

Your family will learn how to study the Bible

You will learn from the Bible in an ongoing family conversation

Pointers for Parents

Listen patiently. Your children's answers are windows into their young hearts. Each discussion is a chance to understand the children you are discipling for Christ.

Use your family Bible. The Bible text is not provided to you for a reason - so that family members open their own Bibles together.

Take breaks. It may be helpful to take a break for a few days or even a week. The idea is to learn, not follow a rigid system or plan.

Help your kids make connections. While there are many moralistic devotional books for children, this Bible study focuses on observation and the author's intent. In this study you will tackle the text section-by-section to underscore the authority of the Bible itself, skipping nothing.

Grow. Allow God to teach/guide/grow *you* in the process of discipling your children.

How Do We Use this Bible study?

Read

In this section, read the Bible passage aloud as a family. Consider changing who reads each passage, or alternate every couple of verses. Keep it fresh!

Talk

This section is not intended to be exhaustive or exhausting. Keep the study moving unless you see the need to slow down for tender hearts that are seeking God.

This section aims to draw out themes or details that might be easily overlooked in a cursory reading.

Pray

The prayer-from-the-heart section gives an opportunity for heart application, encouraging your family to consider: "what should be my heart attitude about this study?"

Sing

Singing in your home, whatever quality it may have, communicates to the next generation that 1) this faith is real, and 2) it is real *to me*. Joyful singing of gospel truth connects scripture to the heart and helps children remember the truth they have been taught.

Each daily suggested hymn in the Family Worship Study is included in the back of this volume with the melody line and chords for use of a family instrument. If you do not know a song, simply read the poetry aloud together!

Extra Time / Activities

Sometimes you may find there is extra time or you want to help your children compare a study's theme with other passages of the Bible. Many of the studies include activities and further study to clarify the truths discussed that day.

Study Length

About 15-20 minutes should be enough time to Read the passage, Talk it through, Pray together, and Sing a few verses from the song for that study.

You know your children. Pace each study to minister to their hearts and develop an awe for God and His Word.

Eight Key Words

Endure, Do, Include, Active, Wisdom, Humility, Treasure, Pray

Memorize the following rhyme to remember the outline of the book of James:

	Section	Theme verse
God helps weak ones to **endure**,	1:2-1:18	1:3
Not merely hear, but **do**, for sure.	1:19-1:27	1:22
Rich and poor **include**d in	2:1-2:13	2:9
The church through **active** faith within.	2:14-2:26	2:17
Wisdom, not just words you need;	3:1-3:18	3:17
Humility, not prideful deeds.	4:1-4:12	4:6
Treasure God, not fragile stuff	4:13-5:12	4:15
Urgent **pray**er when life is rough.	5:13-5:20	5:13

— STUDY #1 —

Before You Get Started...

Theme of the Book: Living faith shows itself by producing true works and by enduring life's trials.

Who wrote James? Traditionally it is believed that Jesus' half-brother, James, wrote this epistle / letter. James would have known the best example of living faith in Jesus while they were growing up in the same home.

To whom did James write? "The 12 tribes scattered" (James 1:1). The epistle was written to Jewish believers scattered throughout the Mediterranean world (1:19; 2:1, 2:7).

When was the book written? 44/45 A.D., likely the first New Testament book written.

What was James' purpose for writing the book? Some believers in the early church failed to put their faith into practice and James encourages Christians not to waver between living for God and living for self.

What is the theme of this book (and this study)? Living faith shows itself by producing true works and by enduring life's trials. Wisdom is an important theme; in fact, James is known as the "Proverbs of the New Testament." James shares wisdom for passionate, living faith.

⇌ OUTLINE OF THE BOOK ⇋

1. Living Faith Endures Trials and Temptations (1:2-1:18)
2. Living Faith Consists of Doing, Not Just Hearing (1:19-1:27)
3. Living Faith Includes Everyone, Not Partiality (2:1-2:13)
4. Living Faith Produces Active, Healthy Spiritual Fruit (2:14-2:26)
5. Living Faith Uses Words Wisely (3:1-3:18)
6. Living Faith Displays Humility, Not Pride (4:1-4:12)
7. Living Faith Treasures God, Not Stuff (4:13-5:12)
8. Living Faith Prays Urgently (5:13-5:20)

** There is a rhyme on page #6 that may help your child remember the outline of this book **

Joy in Trials

📖 **Read:** James 1:1-4

💬 **Talk:**

1. Read verse 3 again. Who do you think allows the "testing of your faith"? *[God allows our faith to be tested]* From v2 how is faith tested? *[with trials of various kinds]* What trials are you facing?

2. What is a trial? *[any difficulty, problem, or hardship in life]* At the end of v3, what do trials produce or grow in our lives? *[Trials produce patience/steadfastness]* What is steadfastness? *[enduring what is unpleasant or difficult without quitting]*

- How does training help you in sports? *[training gives skill, muscle memory, and endurance]* Think of trials like training for life and your walk with God. They train you in endurance and steadfastness to trust God no matter what happens.

- Just like your parents encourage you to do hard or difficult things, **God allows trials in life to teach us** a couple things: 1) to look to Him for help because we are weak or afraid, and 2) to mature and grow us in spiritual endurance.

- Big difference: Parents train you so that one day you will not need them as much; God trains us so that we realize just how much we need Him forever.

3. Because of #1 & #2, **we should actually see trials as God's good work in us**. Ask one of the adults in the room to tell you of a time that God used trials to spiritually grow them and how they see God's good work in them because of the trial.

4. V2 - We can count it all joy. Trials don't mean that God is unhappy with you or wants you to be miserable. When bike tires go flat, when bones break, when trips are canceled, or any other trial, each one is an **opportunity to trust God and grow in your steadfast love for Him**.

5. From v4, the word "perfect" means something a little different. Here, perfect means: *growth of mental and moral character*. Just as your body is growing, God is helping you learn to trust Him in many ways (because of different trials). As your body grows up, remember God is growing your character too. A maturing Christian can have joy in trials because he or she trusts God.

💗 **Pray:** Father, thank You for patiently helping us grow and mature. Help us reflect that same patience back to You as we trust You in the trials we face every day. Teach us to have patient faith and joy in trials. Life can be hard and disappointing, but You are always good.

🎵 **Sing:** How Firm a Foundation (pg 61)

⇟ EXTRA TIME? ⇞

Describe a steadfast person, fictional or real. What did that person believe in and how did that affect their thinking and actions in hard times?

—— STUDY #3 ——

Wisdom from God

📖 **Read:** James 1:5-8

💬 **Talk:**

1. Have you ever been sea sick? The waves on the ocean or lake caused you to feel ill because your body wasn't used to the unstable "ground". Spiritually speaking, a lot of people don't believe confidently in God and James describes how important it is to have God's rock-solid wisdom when you're facing trials.

2. In Study #1 you learned what trials are and how God uses them for good. But when we talk to God about our trials, sometimes we aren't sure what to pray for or even how to handle the difficult situation. God cares about that too. He knows everything about your trial and you can lean on Him for wisdom.

3. What is wisdom? *[allow answers]* **Wisdom means that you can take what you know and make good decisions and judgments.** True wisdom comes from God. In v5, HOW does God give wisdom? *[generously and without hesitation]*

4. V6 instructs us to ask for wisdom in faith. **Faith is a steady confidence in God** based on His words and character. When life becomes difficult for people, the temptation is to doubt God. But when we doubt God, we doubt His character. In truth God is good, loving, wise, and merciful. God has never failed to come through on His promises when the time was right. His character never changes. You can trust Him in a trial and to give you wisdom when you ask in faith, confidently trusting God's Word.

5. From v6, talk about how unstable a wave on the sea is. *[allow discussion]* "Unstable" (opposite of steadfast in v4) describes the person whose mind switches between **faith** in God and **doubt** in God. Can you really act in faith if you're not sure God answers prayer or will actually help? *[discuss]* If you refuse to trust God, can other people ever be sure how you'll react to life? (v8) God is trustworthy; trust Him. Consider the illustration for this study. If the lighthouse represents our faith and the wave represents trials, who helps believers/Christians to confidently trust God in trials? *[God strengthens our faith, helps us trust Him, gives us wisdom. We are powerless; God is mighty]*

❤️ **Pray:** God, you are trustworthy. You are always good, all the time. You love Your people and are merciful toward us every day. When trials come and life is hard, help us choose to trust You regardless how we feel. Give us wisdom to handle trials in a way that honors You. Thank You for giving us wisdom for today.

🎵 **Sing:** How Firm a Foundation (pg 61), also He Will Hold Me Fast (not included in hymn section)

⇟ EXTRA TIME? ⇟

Toss your couch cushions on the floor like a bridge or path. Try walking across them while balancing plastic cups on top of one another. How unstable do you feel?

True Wealth in Jesus

📖 **Read:** James 1:9-11

💬 **Talk:**

1. Throughout history, even today, people are treated differently. Do you know of anyone who was treated well or badly just because they were rich or poor? *[allow answers]* Poverty and wealth make people focus on the world around them rather than on Christ. How should a Christian look at this topic?

2. The Poor

- James says a poor person should boast/glory in his exaltation. What might he be talking about? *[a poor person doesn't own much or have much influence in the world, but he has all the wisdom and riches found in Jesus Christ (Philippians 4:19)]*

- As long as a poor man finds his true worth in Jesus, does he need to feel badly about how few possessions he has? *[no, Jesus defines our worth, not stuff]*

3. The Rich

- James says a rich person should be humble about what he has. Who gives the rich man the ability to earn wealth? *[God]* Does wealth give anyone advantages before God? *[no]*

- How does James illustrate the delicate shortness of life in v10? *[flowers and grass that fade]* What does this mean for the rich man? *[fades away too]*

- As long as a rich man finds his true worth in Jesus, does he have any reason to be proud? *[no, Jesus defines our worth, not stuff]*

- Since a rich person is not better than a poor person, how should a wealthy Christian act toward the poor? *[humble, like an equal, like Jesus acts toward all of us spiritually poor sinners]*

4. The Christian community (your church specifically) is not supposed to act like the world does. How important is money and power to the unbelieving world? *[very important]* The Bible has a lot to say about loving riches more than God. What does Matthew 6:28-34 have to say about wealth? *[seek God and what is important to Him]*

❤️ **Pray:** Father, You have given us everything we need to be content in You. You have promised to provide for us and be our God. Help us trust You no matter how much or how little we have. Teach us to depend on You and to be humble.

🎵 **Sing:** Glorious Things of Thee are Spoken, (pg 60 v4); also Be Thou My Vision (pg 56)

⇟ EXTRA TIME? ⇟
What does it mean that Jesus "became poor"? (look up 2 Corinthians 8:9)

COOKIES

— STUDY #5 —

What is Temptation?

📖 **Read:** James 1:12-18

💬 **Talk:**

1. Have you ever been tempted to eat something disgusting? Something yummy? How about eating too much dessert? How about taking someone else's dessert while they weren't looking?

2. Temptation is the urge to do what is wrong or unwise. **Everyone has been tempted.** Everyone has regretted giving in to temptation.

3. **Temptation reveals your heart.** Temptation comes from your heart's desires.

4. Temptation is an opportunity for decision. You can either turn TO God and grow closer to Him, or you turn AWAY from God to pursue your sinful desires. Following God means everlasting pleasure; following selfish desires only gives temporary pleasure. Every temptation gives an opportunity to love God or self.

5. In Study #1 we saw that God allows us to face trials, but He does not tempt us with evil. Our sinful hearts do that. From God's perspective, trials and hardships are a wonderful opportunity for Him to honor His promises and for Christians to deepen their trust. Our sinful human nature takes a trial or normal desire and turns it into a temptation to sin (v14). Sin is breaking God's law. The Bible tells us everyone has sinned (Romans 3:23).

6. Desiring things like food or comfort is not sin. Being tempted isn't sin. **Giving in to temptation is sin**. Letting your desires rule your life is sin. And sin always brings sorrow or sadness. What are the terrible consequences of sin in v15? *[death is the result of sin]*

7. Who has the power to change our heart's desires? *[God]*

8. Who faced temptation without ever once giving in? *[Jesus]* This is why Jesus alone can save us from the consequences of sin (v15). This is also how **we can hope to avoid giving in to temptation**, because 1) Jesus is with us in temptation and 2) Jesus offers us something more attractive than temptation: Jesus offers us Himself. How? *[allow answers]*

9. How is v17 connected to v9-11? *[further reasons why the temptation to serve wealth is foolish; God has already given me every good thing I need]*

❤️ **Pray:** Lord, help us to love You more than anything. Everything on earth is less attractive when we learn more about You. You are more lovely than the most beautiful thing we can imagine. You are more worthy than anything our hearts might pursue after. Teach our hearts to choose You over our temptations.

🎵 **Sing:** Day by Day (pg 58), or Great Is Thy Faithfulness (not included in hymn section)

⇟ LIVING FAITH LOVES GOD ABOVE ALL ⇞

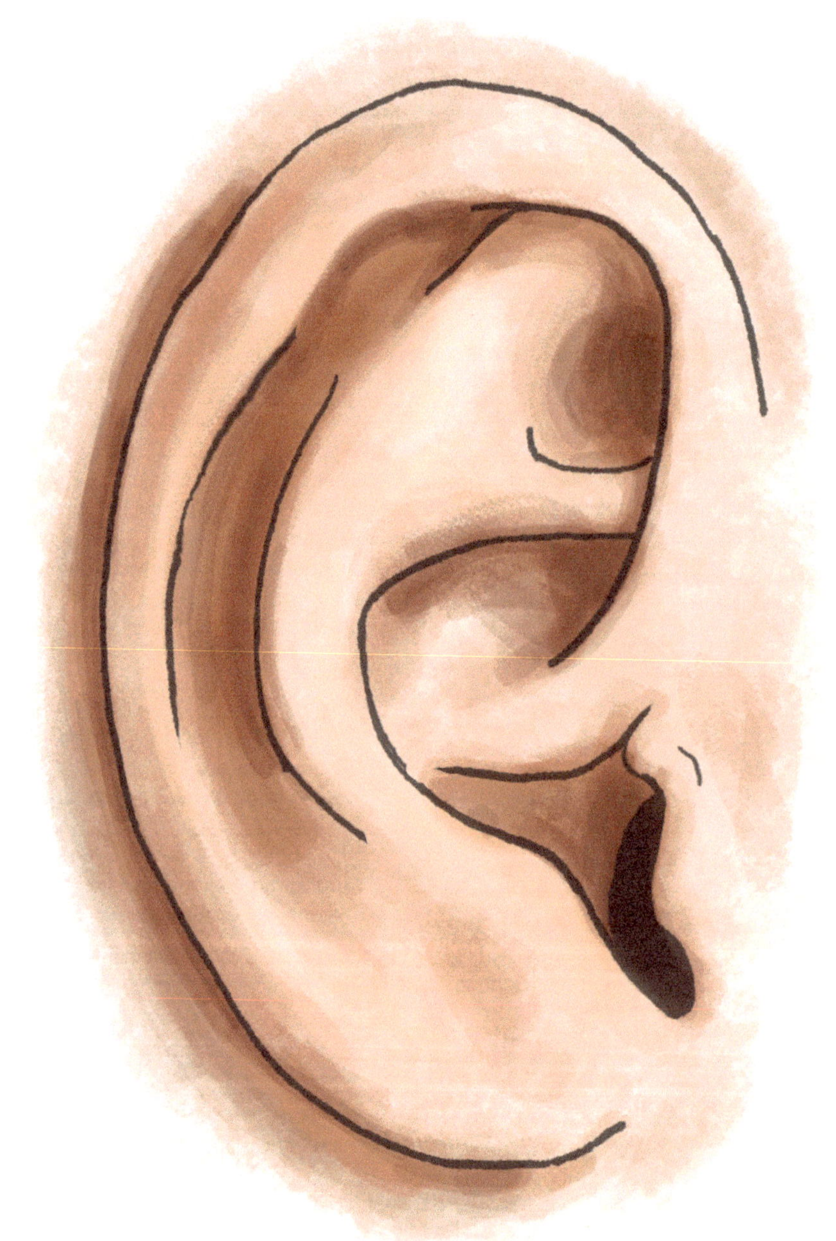

—— STUDY #6 ——

Are You Listening?

📖 **Read:** James 1:19-21

💬 **Talk:**

1. Human beings have five senses; can you name them? *[sight, touch, hear, taste, smell]* As James wrote this letter to Christians, he wanted them to live their faith. It is easy to hear God's Word taught and agree with it. **Living out what we know is more difficult to do.**

2. In v19, we should be quick to do one thing and slow to do two other things. What are they? *[quick:hear, slow:speak/anger]* Most children and adults are quick to speak and quick to be angry. Most people are not very good at listening.

3. Have you ever become angry over something you did not really understand? Many parents have done this, becoming upset at children and declaring punishments before we truly understand what happened. As parents, we regret those times. Why? Because we did not listen fully, decided we knew what happened, then took action far too quickly. In most cases, our relationships were hurt because of being too quick to anger (v20).

4. The Bible tells us that our hearts are deceitful (Jeremiah 17:9). The world tells us to "listen to your heart" and "follow your heart", but God helps us see that our hearts are wicked and deceitful, telling us what is untrue. In v21, the word "meekness" is the opposite of v20. Human anger is proud, stubborn, and does not listen. **Godly wisdom slows down, listens carefully, and tries to help others draw close to God.** When we lose our temper at a brother or sister, does that help them draw close to God? *[no]*

5. Rather than assume you know, ask your friends and family questions. Listen closely. This helps you understand rather than being quick to speak or become angry. Parents, share some of the questions you use to help you understand a situation rather than "jump to conclusions."

❤️ **Pray:** Father, thank you for listening to us. You have promised to hear us when we pray. You never make a rash or harsh decision. Your emotions never rule over your wisdom. Thank you for being Who You are, and help us to become like You: slow to anger, quick to forgive.

🎵 **Sing:** Channels Only (pg 57)

⸕ EXTRA TIME? ⸕

Read Proverbs 16:32 & 14:29. Discuss how self-control is better than physical might and how a quick temper leads to foolishness. Activity: based on v19, try acting out other activities fast and/or slow. Examples: jumping, sneezing, eating, falling. Then read v19 aloud again.

— STUDY #7 —

Don't Forget About It (Fuhgeddaboudit)

📖 **Read:** James 1:22-25

💬 **Talk:**

1. **Living out what we know can be difficult to do.** Study #5 taught us that becoming angry quickly often leads to sin. After you were done with that study, did you become angry with a family member within an hour? Did your anger lead you to sin against someone in your words, thoughts, or actions? God knows that we are quick to agree with His Word, but slow to live out what we know. We forget too easily.

2. In v22, if we hear God's Word but don't do it, what is really happening? *[we are deceived – into thinking we are spiritually healthy]*

3. Look at the picture for this study. Have you ever looked in the mirror and your hair was out of place? Have you ever forgotten to fix your hair and went to school, church, or the store with your hair all crazy? James teaches us in v23 that **people do that same thing when they hear God's Word but fail to do what they have learned.** Hearing God's Word and agreeing with it are good things, but if the way you think, act, or talk never changes, do you really believe God's Word? *[no, real faith changes me]*

4. Read v25 again. For the Christian who "perseveres" and continues to think about God's Word and lets it change his or her life, what does this verse say will happen? *[blessed by Living Faith]*

5. How about you? **Are you a Hearer who forgets or Doer who acts?** No one remembers perfectly, but it is encouraging when you see how God is changing you over time to be a Doer of His Word.

❤️ **Pray:** Lord, help our family to do what You tell us in the Bible. We need Your grace and help to remember all the wonderful things we have learned about You. When we are afraid, help us remember Your presence. When we sin, help us remember your forgiveness. When we are busy, help us to notice all the people with needs all around us. We hear Your Word often; help us to do it too.

🎵 **Sing:** Trust and Obey (pg 66)

DOING, NOT JUST HEARING

⇌ EXTRA TIME? ⇋

As a family, choose a Bible command then act out someone who forgets about God's instruction and someone who remembers. Feel free to have fun with the scenario.

—— STUDY #8 ——

Self Deception

📖 **Read:** James 1:26-27

💬 **Talk:**

1. **Living faith means doing, not just hearing.** In this section of the book (1:19-26) James teaches that Living Faith means doing God's Word and not just hearing it. A lot of people *think* they are believers simply because they know a lot about the Bible. But if the knowledge you have in your head has not changed your heart, then perhaps you are not truly a disciple of Jesus! This is a serious topic!

2. Think of a pure glass of water. It doesn't look cloudy or have floaties in it. V27 says that a person who is a Doer of the Word has pure religion, meaning that he is not a hypocrite, saying one thing and doing the opposite. Pure religion is the same thing as Living Faith: learning about God and letting truth change your life. James gives us three clues what that looks like:

- V26 – **Living faith "reins in" speech.** What animal is a bridle used on? Pigs, whales, or bumblebees? *[no, bridles are for horses]* What does a bridle do? *[controls the powerful horse to obey the rider]* How does bridled speech show that you are under Jesus' control? *[allow answers; when I'm living to please myself I say whatever I want to; when I'm living to please God I am careful what I say and how I say it]*

- V27a – **Living faith shows mercy to the helpless.** There are two groups of people that are mentioned in this verse. Who are they? *[orphans & widows]* In Bible times, orphans and widows often did not have enough food, shelter, or clothes to survive. God cares about people's needs, and Jesus' followers do too. Some people think that the government should take care of people's needs, but the government does not know of all of them. Who has God placed in your life that has needs? Keep your eyes and heart open to notice!

- V27b – **Living faith lives with purity.** Imagine you have a glass of water outside and a dust cloud starts blowing toward you. Would you shield the top of the glass? *[yes, you would cover it to keep it clean]* This verse teaches that Living Faith stays alert to keep clean from the world's way of living and thinking. This does not mean you should hide and never talk to unbelievers. Living purely means that you actively protect your heart. Skip ahead and read James 4:4.

💛 **Pray:** Father, Your loving kindness is shown so clearly by the life of Jesus Christ. Help us become a little more like Jesus today. Teach us to watch our words, open our eyes to see needs, and live godly lives in an evil world.

🎵 **Sing:** Take My Life and Let It Be Consecrated (pg 65)

⇟ **LIVING FAITH HEARS GOD'S WORD THEN DOES IT** ⇟

— STUDY #9 —

Playing Favorites

📖 **Read:** James 2:1-7

💬 **Talk:**

1. What is happening in this picture? *[allow responses]* This illustrates today's text. James teaches that partiality is a sinful attitude. Partiality is favoritism. Who might we be tempted to favor over another person? *[allow answers]* Everyone likes to have a best friend sit next to them on the bus, but what about the child who is "different" that everyone else ignores? Can you think of another example of favoritism / partiality? Ask an adult for help if you need it.

2. An older child or adult: explain what is wrong with the situation in verses 2-3 in your own words. *[sitting in a good place (likely the front) versus standing (in the back) or sitting on the floor (like a servant)]*

3. Christians are not to judge one another like this, playing favorites (v4). Partiality means you set yourself up as the judge, deciding who is worthy of special treatment. Who is the real Judge? *[God]*

4. Sometimes we show favoritism to people we think will bring us advantages but ignore other people because they may make us look bad in public. Disciples of Jesus act like Jesus. Think about the "weird kid" at school... how do you think Jesus would engage with that person? *[loving, patient, interested, welcoming, etc]*

5. Sameness – one of the behaviors of living faith is sameness, or integrity. This means that everywhere you go, you act the same. **You don't change who you are** just to fit in to a certain group. Sameness also means that everywhere you go, **you treat other people the same too**. No matter if others are happy or grumpy, kind or rude, for Christ's sake you treat them all with the same love, gentleness, and consideration. Ask one of the adults about a time when they failed and a time they succeeded at "sameness" and integrity.

INCLUDES EVERYONE

❤️ **Pray:** God, You are our perfect example of integrity. You never change and You judge everyone by the same rule. We confess that each one of us has failed to keep Your law, the law has judged us all guilty, yet you offer us all the same forgiveness through Jesus. Help us see where we play favorites and do not even realize it. Thank you for forgiveness. Help us remember how spiritually poor we were before we knew Christ.

🎵 **Sing:** Channels Only (pg 57)

⇟ EXTRA TIME? ⇞

Compare these Scriptures with today's study: Read Matthew 5:3 and Philippians 2:3 aloud. All disciples of Jesus humbly value others as more important than themselves.

I
II
III
IV
V
VI
VII
VIII
IX
X

— STUDY #10 —

The Royal Law

📖 **Read:** James 2:8-13

💬 **Talk:**

1. Living faith includes everyone without partiality.

2. In v8, the words "royal law" describe life in God's kingdom. Right now, God's kingdom is not physically on earth – it is a spiritual kingdom. But one day in the future, Jesus will bring God's kingdom to earth.

3. If a Christian keeps God's law, everything he/she does will be ruled by God's love. What is it like to try to love everyone all of the time? *[difficult!]* According to v9, what does God think of favoritism? *[it is sin]* Favoritism is not showing love.

4. In v10-11, James teaches that if we break one rule in all of God's law, then we are just as guilty as someone who has broken all of the law.

- Imagine your parent has a gold chain necklace. How many links are in that chain? *[allow answers]* If the necklace breaks, does it matter which link is the broken one in order to call it a 'broken necklace'? *[no, ANY link could break and the necklace cannot be used]*

- In a similar way, breaking one of God's laws makes a person guilty of breaking the law (Romans 3:23). Breaking even one link means the whole is broken.

5. V12-13 takes some thinking.

- James gives a different name to the law in v12. What is it? *[law of liberty]* People think they are free if there are no rules or authority, but that is not freedom. Since mankind's worst bondage is to sin, then real freedom means being set free from the power of sin. Who has the power to do that? *[God/Jesus]* The gospel of Jesus Christ has the power to set us truly free from sin.

- Read Micah 6:8. V13 is a summary of verses 1-12. Playing favorites and showing mercy are opposites. How did Jesus treat the poor? *[merciful]* If you want to be like Jesus, show mercy toward others, seeing them with spiritual eyes rather than deciding someone's worth with your physical eyes. Read Acts 3:1-10 as an example of Christlike mercy.

❤ **Pray:** Heavenly Father, You are the perfect example of loving every person the same. You offer salvation to everyone. Thank You. Your law is not about keeping rules, but the law of liberty has taught us today that loving You means loving others. Help us to learn Your heart.

🎵 **Sing:** Trust and Obey (pg 66), or The Law of the Lord Is Perfect (Joanne R. Graham, not in hymn section)

⇌ EXTRA TIME? ⇌

If time allows, read or summarize Luke 10:25-37. From this parable, how important is it to God that you show others the same love, mercy, etc that He has show to you?

JAMES: LIVING FAITH

— STUDY #11 —

Warmed & Filled

Read: James 2:14-17

Talk:

1. If a person has living faith, then that person's actions will show it. If a friend claims to be athletic but never wants to run or play, do you think they are being honest? *[no]* If a person claims to be an artist but never draws, paints or chisels anything, is their claim honest? *[no]* What about a person who claims to have faith but does not act like Christ?
2. In Studies 8-9 James taught how living faith includes everyone without favoritism, because this is what it means to live for God without hypocrisy (saying one thing but doing the opposite). Now in Studies 10-12 James teaches that living faith actually produces spiritual fruit. An apple tree that never bears any fruit is useless; a Christian who does not act like Jesus is not being fruitful either. Which tree in the drawing is being fruitful?
3. V14 asks us to think about having real, living faith, not faking it. Read v15-16 again. Who is the "brother or sister" talking about? *[other people, especially other Christians]* What are their needs in v15? *[good clothing and food]* In v16, does the person speaking want good things for this brother or sister? *[yes]* But does the person speaking actually do anything about those needs? *[no]* What do you think of this response to someone in need? *[allow responses]*
4. V17 gives the main point. Read it aloud. When you see someone with needs and your heart feels compassion for them, but you do nothing to help, James asks "What good is that?!" When you plant an apple tree that never gives any fruit, you ask "What good is that?!" When a person claims to be a Christian and a follower of Jesus but never produces spiritual fruit, then James is asking again "What good is that?!"
5. Why is it important that people who claim to follow and love Jesus learn how to think and act and live like Jesus did? In what ways did Jesus back up His words with action? What needs do you see in your home/church/neighborhood?

Pray: Lord you are never fake or unaware of our needs. You saw our heart's greatest need and took action, providing rescue from our sins. We want to follow Your example. Give us eyes that see needs and courage to live out our faith.

Sing: Jesus, What a Friend for Sinners (pg 62), also Wonderful Merciful Savior (not included in hymn section)

LIVING FAITH SEES BOTH SPIRITUAL & PHYSICAL NEEDS

—— STUDY #12 ——

Useless 'Faith'

📖 **Read:** James 2:18-20

💬 **Talk:**

1. Have you ever answered a question before it was asked? James does this in today's study.
2. V18 – The question James answers is: "James, why can't you be the one who has works and I be the one who has faith? Why do I have to have *both*?" **Some people think that faith will save them without changing how they live their life.** In other words, some people think they can fill their brains with knowledge about God and that means they are a Christian, a disciple of Jesus.
3. V19 - Do you know the *shema*, the Jewish creed? Read Deuteronomy 6:4. James is writing to early Christians, most of whom were Jewish. In order to teach a lesson, he uses this familiar creed that most of his readers would know. The statement from Deuteronomy declares that there is only one God.
   - Does James say that believing the *shema* is a good thing or bad thing *[good]*
   - From this verse, who else believes there is one God? *[demons believe this truth too]*

- So what is the difference between demonic belief and saving faith? *[believing God exists does not mean you are forgiven by God; saving faith trusts in Jesus for salvation]*
4. What are some wonderful things God tells us about Himself in the Bible? *[allow answers]* You can study these things, memorize them, and believe them to be true – but if your heart toward God does not change, then (like was asked in Study #10) "what good is that?!" **This is useless "faith."** Truly, if God has given you the gift of salvation by faith in Jesus, your life will definitely change, especially how you treat others.
5. The demons, who believe God's Word to be true, do not have faith toward God. **When your heart believes God's Word in faith, then your life cannot remain the same.** Your heart, thoughts, words, actions, and everything begins to change over time. If you say you have faith and your actions never change to look like Jesus', then James says in v20 that your so-called faith is useless! Those are pretty strong words to think about.

❤️ **Pray:** Father, You have told us many wonderful things about Yourself in the Bible. Teach us to live for You like Jesus Christ, serving and loving You and others each day. Help us to walk through life with You and not just learn about You. Father, let living faith change my heart and life.

🎵 **Sing:** How Firm a Foundation (pg 61), or Trust and Obey (pg 66)

⸎ EXTRA TIME? ⸎

Take three minutes to quietly reflect (think about) your relationship to others in your family. Is your faith active? Does your faith match the way you act toward them?

— STUDY #13 —

Your Faith is Showing

📖 **Read:** James 2:21-26

💬 **Talk:**

1. How do you know for certain that a fruit tree is either an apple tree or a pear tree? *[allow answers; taste the ripe fruit]* How do you know if a dessert is good or gross? *[taste it]* How do you know if a chair is sturdy? *[convince your friend to sit in it first]* If you want to know for certain, eventually you must test the fruit, or dessert, or chair, to see its quality. Eventually, everything shows its quality, including our faith when it is tested. Fully-grown, mature and living faith shows itself in how we live.

2. *Abraham showed his faith by his actions/works – v21-24*

   - Read Genesis 22:7-13 (also Hebrews 11:17-19)

   - How did Abraham show faith in God by offering Isaac to God as a sacrifice? *[obeyed God's command even if it did not make sense at the time; willing to give up the son God promised him many years before]*

   - If Abraham did NOT have faith in God, how might his actions/works have been different? *[would never have risked Isaac's life, believing instead that God was asking him to give up too much]*

3. *Rahab showed her faith by her actions/works – v25-26*

   - Read Hebrews 11:30-31

   - How did Rahab show faith in God by protecting the spies sent into Jericho? *[she chose to help God's people rather than oppose God's plan for Israel]*

   - If Rahab did NOT have faith in God, how might her actions/works have been different? *[she would have called for Jericho's guards to arrest the two spies, believing instead that her false Canaanite gods would help them against the Hebrew God]*

4. *Do you see how faith and works must go together?* It is true that no one can work his way to heaven (Galatians 2:16). It is also true that faith shows itself in how a person acts (James 2:24).

5. Is your faith showing? Do you have living faith? Ask an adult to share a time that they showed living faith, taking what they know about God and acting on it.

❤️ **Pray:** God, please show our family how to live our faith. When you give us commands in Your Word, help us obey. When you warn us to live wisely, help us avoid foolishness. As we understand Your love, help us see to whom we should show Your love. We want our faith in You to show as we live for You each day.

🎵 **Sing:** When I Survey the Wondrous Cross (pg 67 v4); also, By Faith (Getty, not included in hymn section)

⇌ FULLY-GROWN, MATURE & LIVING FAITH SHOWS ITSELF IN HOW WE LIVE ⇌

JAMES: LIVING FAITH

STUDY #14

Horses & Ships

Read: James 3:1-5a

Talk:

1. How big is the largest ship you have ever seen? Have you ever taken a ride on a horse? James teaches about our words in this study, and he uses horses and ships to show how important our words can be.
2. V1 - James noticed that a lot of people in the early church were eager to teach, to speak up and explain what they knew about God. Does James encourage this, or warn these people? *[warns them to be careful]* Why should teachers be careful? *[because people must teach God's truth, not their own opinions; God holds teachers accountable]* Compare this to James 1:19.
3. V2 - The word "perfect" is the same word used in 1:4, meaning "complete, growing into maturity." It does not mean "flawless" or "without sin." James is teaching in this section (Studies 13-15) that **living faith learns to use words wisely.**
4. V3-4 - Why do horses have bridles? *[to control them]* A little bridle guides a big animal! Why do ships have a rudder? *[to control the ship's direction]* A little thing like a rudder guides a big ship in the sea!
5. V5 - What small part of the human body does James talk about in this verse? *[the tongue]* What do we use our tongues for? *[taste and talking]* Our words are important because they have the power to help or hurt others. Read v2 again. A wise person who is living out her faith understands that her words are important. Some people think they are free when they can say whatever they feel like saying. Would James agree with this? *[no]* Rather than trying to be "free", a maturing Christian does not say whatever she wants to say. Instead she uses her words to help others know and love God.
6. Does your tongue speak proud words? Harmful words? Do you talk back to your parents or insult your brother or sister? Words can do powerful harm. They can also be a powerful help. The tongue is very small, but has a big impact.

Pray: Lord, rule over our thoughts and words. We confess that too many times our words and attitudes do not sound or look like Jesus. Teach us self control, and to understand how important our words are.

Sing: Channels Only (pg 57)

EXTRA TIME?

Read Galatians 5:22-24. How does the fruit of the Spirit show living faith?

— STUDY #15 —

Fire, Water & Figs

📖 **Read:** James 3:5b-12

💬 **Talk:**

1. **Living faith uses words wisely.** In the verses for today, James uses strong word pictures to help us understand the danger of uncontrolled words and tone. The words you choose are "what" you say; how you say those words is the "tone" of your words. How many different ways (tones) can you say the words, "Hi Grandma"? *[excited, sarcastic, bored, fearful, cheerful]* **What** you say and **How** you say it are very important to God.

2. Read v5b-6 again. What word picture does James use to describe the tongue? *[fire that becomes out of control]* Perhaps you think of a house burning or a forest fire. The tongue can do great harm by spreading rumors, lying to authorities, or tearing someone down with words. Is it easy to use our words to harm others? *[yes, too easy]* Christians must not use our words this way; in fact, that is one of the important ways that unbelievers see Jesus in us – by grace-filled speech.

3. The tongue cannot be tamed (v7-8). Name an animal that has been tamed by humans. People have found ways to tame animals, but the tongue always seems wild and unpredictable. Can you think of anyone who has only ever used their words in a good way? Not one person on the earth and in history has had perfect control of his or her tongue (except Jesus). Why does everyone struggle to control their words and tone?

- This is because our words and our thoughts come from our hearts (Matthew 12:34)

- ... and our hearts are desperately wicked (Jeremiah 17:9)

4. How else does v8 describe the words that come from our hearts? *[deadly poison]*

5. It is hypocrisy to bless God while cursing other people. V9-10 describe two kinds of speech coming from the same person's heart. What are they? *[blessing God/cursing others]* Should this kind of hypocrisy happen (saying one thing and doing the opposite)? *[no!]* In your own words, explain how James illustrates this point with water and fruit trees.

❤️ **Pray:** You are our Creator. You made us to bring you praise and to tell the truth about all of life. But this is not what we do, Lord. Many times we fail to build each other up. Forgive our proud words and patiently teach us grow up in living faith, using our tongues the bless everyone You bring into our lives.

🎵 **Sing:** Take My Life and Let It Be Consecrated (pg 65)

⇥ LIVING FAITH USES WORDS WISELY ⇤

─── STUDY #16 ───

Heavenly Wisdom

📖 **Read:** James 3:13-18

💬 **Talk:**

1. **Living faith uses words wisely.** Study #13 pointed out that the tongue is very small but boasts big things. Study #14 helped you see how the same mouth speaks opposites because our words come from our hearts. Everywhere we go and whoever we are with, we need God's Word and self-control to use our words wisely.

2. V13-14 were written toward the same people who wanted to be authorities and teachers in James 3:1. Some people are gifted to be really good teachers. Who is or was your favorite teacher and why? *[allow answers]* Sometimes a gifted teacher can become proud and arrogant, even a Bible teacher. Meekness (strength under control) was considered a weakness in the ancient world; Jesus considered it super important (Matthew 5:5). *When you are secure in who God made you, you do not have to promote yourself and compete with other people for importance.* Godly wisdom is meek.

- Really smart people help the world by figuring out problems and inventing new things. However, what happens when the smartest kid in class begins to act proud and arrogant because they KNOW they are the smartest? *[no one likes that at all]* The same thing happens with athletic and good-looking people too.

- Worldy wisdom says: *"If you have a skill, promote yourself so everyone knows how awesome you are."* But this is not God's way.

- Heavenly, godly wisdom says: *"God has given me skills so I can use them to glorify God (make Him famous) and bless the people around me."* Godly wisdom is humble and meek, just like Jesus.

- Godly wisdom points other people to God. Describe what might be going on in the illustration for this study. Is this young man trying to glorify himself or to glorify God? *[God]* Are you ready to point other people to God too?

3. **Activity Alert:** Find a piece of scrap paper and write down all the ways that worldy wisdom shows itself in v15-16. You should list around seven. Then, list all the ways that godly wisdom shows itself from v17-18, about eight ways. Choose a skill God has given one of you and discuss how a person uses that skill in both worldly wisdom and heavenly wisdom.

❤️ **Pray:** Father, You have made us in Your image, in many ways similar to Yourself. Take every skill and every dream that we have and bend them to Your will. We will not push to have our own way, but that Your will would be done in our lives. Help us work hard for You, not for our own fame.

🎵 **Sing:** Glorious Things of Thee Are Spoken (pg 60), or I Would Be Like Jesus (not included in hymn section)

⇟ EXTRA TIME? ⇟

What is a troubling situation you face? How might you be tempted toward worldly wisdom (v14-16)? How do v17-18 guide you toward heavenly wisdom in this situation?

—— STUDY #17 ——

Proud Enemy of God

 **Read:** James 4:1-6

Talk:

1. Studies #13-15 explained that people often compete with their words, promoting self. The next two studies explain the heart attitude behind selfish competition: pride.

2. Describe what is going on in this illustration. *[argument/fighting]* What do you think caused this fight? *[allow answers]* **Somebody wanted** something, **but** *something else stopped that from happening,* **so** *a fight broke out.* This happens very often, and not just to children. Adults do this too. Husbands and wives, coworkers, and holiday shoppers. This is the pattern: Somebody – Wanted – But – So…

3. In v1, where does James say that arguments come from? *[desires/passions]* Sometimes people passionately desire evil things; this is obviously bad. Other times people desire good things, but try to get those good things in selfish ways and for selfish reasons. If we love God, we should want the right things and then work toward those things the right way, God's way.

4. Verses 2-3 basically say: "You want some things so badly, you sin to get them. Then, if you still cannot have what you want, you make everyone else miserable because you're upset. Your desires are unmet because you don't ask God, but even when you do ask God you're asking selfishly for your own benefit." Does James sound exasperated? (ask an adult to define that word) From v4, if we live by every selfish passion that comes from our hearts, how does that affect our relationship to God? *[we act like an enemy of God, as though we were never His child in the first place]*

5. Read v6 again. What is the action that God is taking toward the proud and humble? *[opposes/ gives grace]* How does pride and humility look in family relationships? (spouse, siblings, etc)

Pray: Lord, even though You are the Creator and the most important, powerful Person in the universe, Your heart is humble. You showed us this in the life of Jesus. He left heaven's glory to come to this lowly earth. He did not look to promote Himself, but the Father. He set aside His needs and desires in order to help the people around Him, because that was Your desire. Help us learn what You want and then lovingly, humbly pursue those things.

Sing: Fairest Lord Jesus (pg 59) or Seek Ye First (not included in hymn section)

⨪ EXTRA TIME? ⨪

Discuss how Proverbs 13:10 agrees with James 4:1.

—— STUDY #18 ——

Humble Servant of God

📖 **Read:** James 4:7-12

💬 **Talk:**

DISPLAYS HUMILITY

1. What does "submit" mean? *[placing yourself willingly under an authority]* Based on v6 and Study #17, what kind of person do you think submits to God. *[humble person]*

2. Far & Near: In v7, whose power and influence moves far away from a humble servant of God? *[the devil]* In v8, whose power and influence is brought near to a humble servant of God? *[God's]* Many times we pray for God to be near us when we are scared or in trouble. Do you ever stop to think that maybe God seems far from you because you might have been acting full of pride? *[allow time to think]* How might the word "doubleminded" be connected to James 3:11? *[much of this letter talks about people trying to have life both ways, serving self and serving God, but it does not work]* Connected to James 1:6-8? *[not fully trusting God, easily forgets what is true]*

3. V10 – Rather than proudly promoting yourself and all the things you want, God teaches you to be humble. When we focus on glorifying God, we do not have to argue or fight with other people to get what we want. We leave it up to God.

4. Remember in 3:1, some Christians really wanted to be the authority, the teacher. James warned them about the big responsibility that teaching is. Now in 4:11-12, James points out that people try to be the judge, deciding if all the people around them are right or wrong. Adults, give some examples how people judge one another by their own standards. Who is the only true Judge that v12 is talking about? *[God Himself is the only one with authority to judge people by His Word]*

5. Humility sees other people as valuable. Humility realizes, *"I am not perfect and mess up too."* Humility encourages others to be better in a cheerful tone. Humility remembers that God is God, and I am not God. Is your heart submitted to God?

❤️ **Pray:** Father, we will wait for You. All of our desires and dreams, the things we really want, we gladly give up. Love and truth come from You; selfishness and pride come from our hearts. Every day we show our pride and yet You love and forgive us over and over. What a wonderful God You are!

🎵 **Sing:** May the Mind of Christ My Savior (pg 63), or I Run to Christ (not included in hymn section)

⇟ EXTRA TIME? ⇞

Read Philippians 2:5-8. Look for the words Jesus/servant/humble. Then compare 2:9 to James 4:10. Do these verses agree with each other? Our job is to be humble; God does the exalting. Can you think of actions for verses 7-10?

Big Plans (boasting about tomorrow)

📖 **Read:** James 4:13-17

💬 **Talk:**

1. This study and the next two will teach that living faith treasures God, not stuff.

2. Treasure Talk: What does a pirate treasure? *[gold]* What does a squirrel treasure? *[acorns]* A musician? Architect? How about you: what do you treasure? *[allow responses]* Human beings treasure all kinds of things: food, possessions, comfort, power, money, and more. Above anything else, Christians treasure God.

3. Bad Big Plan: What is the plan in v13? *[go to a town and make a lot of money in business]* Does it sound like anyone asked God's opinion about the plan? *[no]* In v14, what does James compare our lives to? *[mist/vapor]* Have you watched steam rise from a mug of hot chocolate or hot tea? How far does the steam rise until it disappears? Can you ever get the steam back? **Life is like a vapor that does not last very long.** (see illustration)

4. Humble Plan: What does v15 give as a better attitude? *[humbly remembers that without God's blessing, the best plans are not good enough]* Notice this important point: making plans is not the problem, but boasting with certainty that YOUR plan is failproof and that YOU alone are smart – this proud boasting is the problem.

Making a plan is a wise, good thing to do. Forgetting God in your life is a foolish thing to do. Name some of your family's plans. Do any of them need to change?

5. People have existed on earth for thousands of years, but we each only live a short time. *If we live apart from God*, we live life selfishly and desperately. *If we are God's child*, we live wisely, unselfishly, and peacefully. **Be sure to make a plan, but do not boast about tomorrow.** Whatever your heart treasures, remember that nothing matters more than God.

6. Consider this poem by CT Studd:
   Two little lines I heard one day,
   Traveling along life's busy way;
   Bringing conviction to my heart,
   And from my mind would not depart;
   Only one life, 'twill soon be past,
   Only what's done for Christ will last.
   Only one life, a few brief years,
   Each with its burdens, hopes, and fears;
   Each with its clays I must fulfill.
   living for self or in His will;
   Only one life, 'twill soon be past,
   Only what's done for Christ will last.

❤️ **Pray:** God, we submit our plans to You. Wherever You want us to go and whatever You want us to do – that will be our plan. Our lives are too short to spend life treasuring things that do not last.

🎵 **Sing:** Be Thou My Vision (pg 56), also Be Unto Your Name (not included in hymn section)

⇒ LIVING FAITH SUBMITS TO GOD'S PLAN ⇐

— STUDY #20 —

Look Out (warning to the rich)

📖 **Read:** James 5:1-6

💬 **Talk:**

1. Does your school have any special jobs for older or responsible students to fulfill? Some schools have student government, or hall monitors, or "safeties" that help the younger kids cross the parking lot. Have you ever seen a student use his or her position to boss people around? *[allow answers]* In chapter 5, James begins by confronting some people who were abusing their position and taking advantage of others. Confronting means he was not going to let them get away with doing wrong.

2. In the Roman Empire much of the land was owned by wealthy businesspeople. James uses very strong language and word pictures to confront their wrongdoing. As you read this section, did you understand their sin?

   • They greedily stored up money for themselves (v2-3, 5)

   • They lied to field workers, paying less than promised (v4)

   • They ignored the pleas and requests for help (v4)

   • They treasured stuff and not God

3. As people build wealth and riches, they can think things like, "I deserve this money more than the workers because I'm the boss." Or "They should have known I was playing games with their pay; they're just easy to trick." But God does not give people wealth so that they can be selfish with it. God blesses people with wealth so they can bless others with it.

4. V4 – "reached the ears of the Lord of Hosts" This warning means that God heard the cries of abused workers. The name "Lord of Hosts" is an Old Testament picture of God as a warrior King going to battle. Would you want to be in battle against God? *[no!]*

5. Parents, share the testimony of a Christian businessperson you know who used his or her position and influence to bless other people, grow an honest business, and honor God with their talents. Perhaps one of the children studying this passage today will become a godly businessperson who resists temptation and chooses to love their workers.

❤️ **Pray:** Father, Your grace and mercy are greater than our sin. We rebel against You, choose our own way, break Your law, and live like we are in charge. We deserve eternal punishment for the way we act toward You, but You lovingly, justly offer us Rescue. We do not deserve Your mercy or patience. Since you have loved us like this, help us love others so they know Your love too.

🎵 **Sing:** Fairest Lord Jesus (pg 59)

— STUDY #21 —

Patience in Suffering

📖 **Read:** James 5:7-12

💬 **Talk:**

1. What is the name of a worker who places seeds in the ground? *[farmer]* Does a farmer plant a seed one day and then hope for fruit the next day? *[no]* Why not? *[plants take time/patience to grow]* Farming takes patience. James says that waiting for Jesus takes patience too.

2. From v7, the early and late rains fell at the beginning and end of the growing season. In Palestine the early rain came just after seeds were planted; the late rain came just before harvest. These rains were important for a successful crop. Between the early and late rain there was a lot of work to do for the farmer. There is also a lot of work to do between the first time Jesus came and the time He returns (v8).

3. V9 – How do you respond when you have to wait a long time for something? *[impatient/grumpy]* When people are suffering or facing hardship (James 1:2,12), they sometimes turn on each other and attack each other.

4. V10-11 James reminds us of all of the Old Testament prophets that patiently served God in tough circumstances. Which one does he name? *[Job]* How did Job wait patiently on God during his suffering? *[trusted God and refused to accuse God]* How did God reward Job? *[rewarded his faithfulness, especially with a better knowledge of God Himself]*

5. This section of the book teaches that living faith treasures God, not stuff. How does suffering and hardship keep us from treasuring life here on earth too much? *[allow answers]*

❤️ **Pray:** Lord, thank You for Your purposes. You do not make any mistakes and Your plans are always good. They cannot be anything other than good. May we learn patience, and stop being angry when life is hard. Help us grow through hardships and know Your love more and more.

🎵 **Sing:** My Shepherd Will Supply My Need (pg 64)

⇔ LIVING FAITH TRUSTS GOD FAITHFULLY OVER TIME ⇔

— STUDY #22 —

Pray About Everything

📖 **Read:** James 5:13-18

💬 **Talk:**

1. The final section of the book of James shows that living faith is urgent. What does it mean if a situation is 'urgent'? *[understanding that a situation needs immediate action]* What are some examples of urgent situations? *[car accident, baby about to be born, message for a general in battle]*

- Some people act urgently about everything. This kind of person does everything as though it is super duper important. Even small things, like eating oatmeal, can be urgent to this person (haha).

2. Read v13-14 again. What are the three examples James gives as good times to pray? *[when someone is suffering, cheerful, or sick]* **In other words, Christians should pray about everything.** When life is good or hard, pray. Talk to God about your life.

3. V15 can be tricky to understand. Sometimes when a person is very sick, they may call for a pastor or elder to come pray with him. Simply asking a pastor to visit in the hospital does not mean that the person will get better every time. "Anointing with oil" in the Old Testament was an expression of dependence on the Spirit of God. There was nothing magic about using oils. Here are truths we know:

- Many people put their faith in Jesus in the last years or days of their life.

- Some people's stubborn hearts are tender to the gospel when they are very sick or near death. They call out to the Lord and He hears them (Psalm 34:4-6).

- When people are injured or unwell, visitors can be encouraging, especially when the visitor points them to God together in prayer.

4. Which Old Testament prophet is named in v17-18? *[Elijah]* In the account from 1 Kings 17-18, Elijah prays for rain to stop (remember early/late rain from Study #20) and no rain fell for how long? *[3 years and 6 months]* Elijah prayed in response to God's Word (Deuteronomy 28:22; 1 Kings 18:1) What does that illustrate for us (hint: v16b)? *[the prayer of righteous people]* Prayer is effective because: **1) God is the One who answers prayer** (Ephesians 3:20) and **2) living faith continues to pray urgently** (Luke 18:1-8; Mark 7:24-30).

❤️ **Pray:** Father, thank You for hearing our prayer. We come to You with our happy times and sad times, knowing You care about them all. We know so many other people who need Your salvation and need Your grace in their suffering.

🎵 **Sing:** Day by Day (pg 58)

⇣ EXTRA TIME? ⇣

Discuss what it means to pray urgently. Is it simply an emotion? A body position? Is it the heart-attitude?

Loving the Wanderer

📖 **Read:** James 5:19-20

💬 **Talk:**

1. What is going on in this study's illustration? *[allow responses]* A shepherd **watches over** a flock of sheep, **leading** them to good grass and water. A shepherd **looks out for danger** as well, **protecting** the sheep and **keeping** them safe. Who is the Good Shepherd (John 10:11,14)? *[Jesus Christ]* How do pastors act like shepherds toward the church? *[look at bold words above]* Your pastor is an under-shepherd, helping you and your church family follow the Good Shepherd.

2. Sometimes people wander from the truth. Parents help their children learn truth and then remind those children a zillion times until they are grown. Adults can wander from the truth too, which is why we need the church and an under-shepherd. Below are some truths we see in v19-20. Take the time to read the cross references aloud.

- Anyone can forget the truth and act like someone that does not know God (Psalm 78:7).

- Christians love each other by bringing someone back to the Good Shepherd, away from danger, lies, and faithless living (Psalm 103:2-3,8-13).

- Only the Good Shepherd (Jesus) forgives sin (Luke 5:24; Luke 1:16).

- Other sheep (Christians) can lead a wandering believer back to a right relationship with God (Galatians 6:1-2).

- When we lovingly confront one another, we help to avoid more sin and faithless living (Proverbs 27:17).

3. There are many ways to love the wanderer, but a good one is urgent prayer like in Study #21. Think about it: anywhere you are, and at any time, **you can pray for someone who has wandered from the Good Shepherd**. Sometimes a Christian looks for the wanderer until they are found and reminds them of the Lord and His love, but all the time a church can pray urgently for each other to stay walking close to God in Living Faith.

❤️ **Pray:** Heavenly Father, all of us tend to forget You and wander away. We want to stay close to You but are easily distracted and tempted to love other things than You. At all times, help us remember our Savior, Jesus Christ, and the love He showed us on the cross. Give us courage to confront one another to stay close to the Good Shepherd.

🎵 **Sing:** Channels Only (pg 57)

PRAYS URGENTLY

⇀ **LIVING FAITH LOVES OTHERS** ↽

DO
INCLUDE
ACTIVE
ENDURE
LIVING FAITH
WISDOM
PRAY
TREASURE
HUMILITY

— STUDY #24 —

Eight Tests of True Faith

📖 **Read:** Various Passages

💬 **Talk:** How do we know if we have living faith? Spiritually speaking, there are eight tests that outline everything in the letter from James.

1. 1:2-18 *Living Faith endures trials and temptation (theme verse: 1:3)*

   - Do you trust God or doubt God when life is hard?

   - Do you ask God for help and wisdom rather than looking to yourself for answers?

2. 1:19-27 *Living Faith does the Word of God (theme verse: 1:22)*

   - When you hear God's Word taught, does it stop at your head or does it reach your heart?

   - How do you see the Word of God changing what you do and say?

3. 2:1-13 *Living Faith includes everyone without partiality (theme verse: 2:9)*

   - In the last couple of weeks, have you been cruel or left people out?

   - In what ways are you tempted to play favorites?

4. 2:14-26 *Living Faith produces healthy spiritual fruit (theme verse: 2:17)*

   - Have you been praying for God to help you see the needs of others?

   - If you claim to follow and love Jesus, are you learning how to think and act and live like Jesus did?

5. 3:1-18 *Living Faith acts and speaks with wisdom (theme verse: 3:17)*

   - How does your speech show others God's wisdom?

   - Do your words and tone of voice show selfishness and pride, or patience and love?

6. 4:1-12 *Living Faith displays humility, not pride (theme verse: 4:6)*

   - By your actions and attitude, do you act like a proud enemy of God or a humble servant of God?

7. 4:13-5:12 *Living Faith treasures God, not stuff (theme verse: 4:15)*

   - Do your big plans include God's will or do you focus only on what you want?

   - Is your heart focused on material things that don't last long, or on spiritual things that last for eternity?

   - Do you remember that suffering is only temporary and that your relationship with God is forever?

8. 5:13-18 *Living Faith responds to all of life with urgent prayer (theme verse: 5:13)*

   - When a bad day keeps getting worse, do you turn to God in prayer first, or turn to yourself to fix things?

   - Do you see yourself as a person God can use to show His love toward others?

Family Harmony

Singing in your home, whatever quality it may have, communicates to the next generation that 1) this faith we speak of is real, and 2) it is real to the parents and adults in the room.

Joyful singing of gospel truth after each study helps connect scripture to the heart. The very best hymns and songs we can sing are those that bring Scripture to mind!

The songs in this collection are familiar to many and produced for you to use. There may be songs familiar to your family that come to mind during the course of the study, and choosing to sing that song may have great benefit too.

If a song in this collection is unfamiliar, consider reading the poetry aloud. Scan the QR code to sing or play along with the song for each study.

About that singing voice...

Someone once said, "Christian music is the intersection of truth and beauty." While you may not feel that your singing voice conveys beauty, children love to hear their parents and grandparents sing anyway.

Chords are included so the family guitar, ukulele or balalaika can be incorporated in worship.

Be Thou My Vision

My flesh and my heart may fail, but God is the strength of
my heart and my portion forever. Psalm 73:26

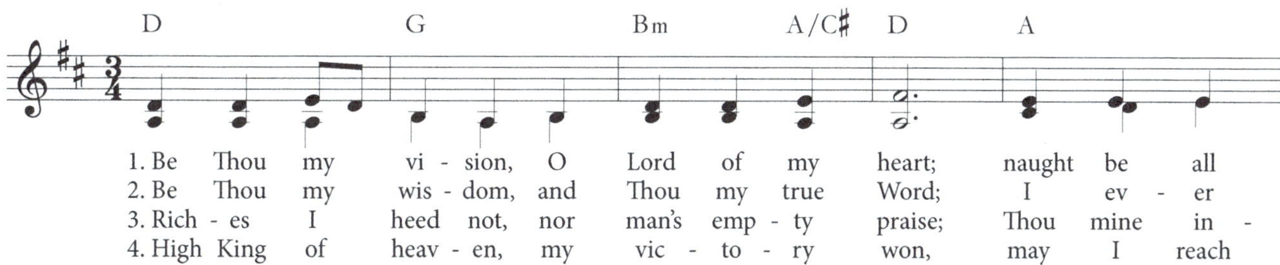

TEXT: 8th-century hymn, trans. Mary Elizabeth Byrne, vers. Eleanor Hull, 1912
MUSIC: Irish folk melody

SLANE
10.10.10.10

Channels Only

Therefore, if anyone cleanses himself from what is dishonorable, he will be a vessel for honorable use,
set apart as holy, useful to the master of the house, ready for every good work.   2 Timothy 2:21

TEXT: Mary E. Maxwell 1900, alt.
MUSIC: Ada R. Gibbs 1900

CHANNELS

Day by Day

By day the LORD commands his steadfast love, and at night his song is with me,
a prayer to the God of my life.   Psalm 42:8

TEXT: Carolina Sandell, 1865. TRANSLATION: A.L. Skoog
MUSIC: Carolina Sandell

BLOTT EN DAG

Fairest Lord Jesus

You are fairer than the sons of men... therefore God has blessed You forever. Psalm 45:2

TEXT: *Muenster Gesangbuch*, 1677
MUSIC: Silesian folk melody, *Schleische Volkslieder*, 1842

CRUSADERS' HYMN
56.85.58

Glorious Things of Thee Are Spoken

The Lord loves the gates of Zion more than all the other dwelling places of Jacob.
Glorious things are spoken of you, O city of God! Psalm 87:2-3

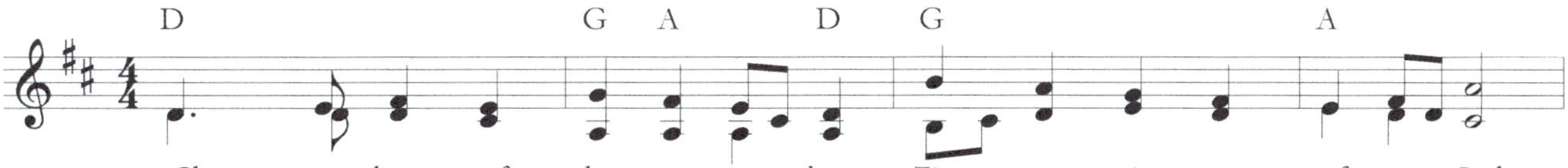

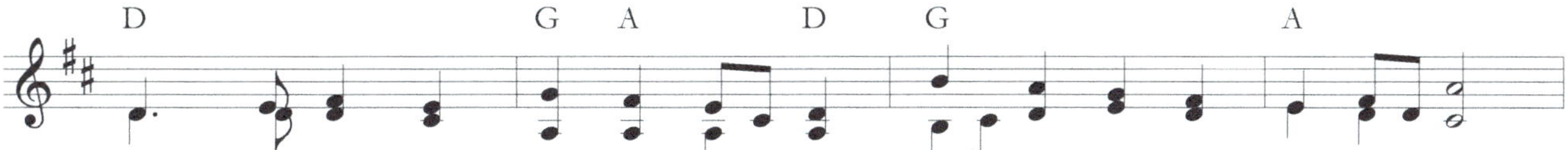

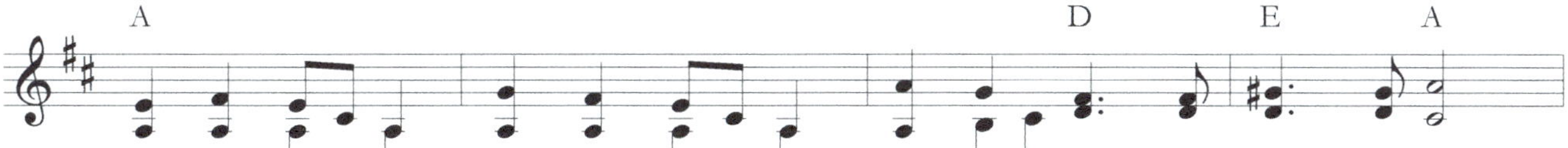

TEXT: John Newton, 1779, alt.
MUSIC: Franz Joseph Haydn, 1797

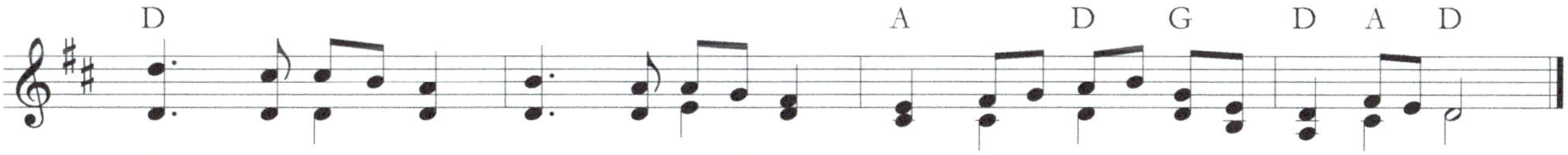

AUSTRIAN HYMN

How Firm a Foundation

Fear not, for I am with you; be not dismayed, for I am your God; I will strengthen you,
I will help you, I will uphold you with My righteous right hand. Isaiah 41:10

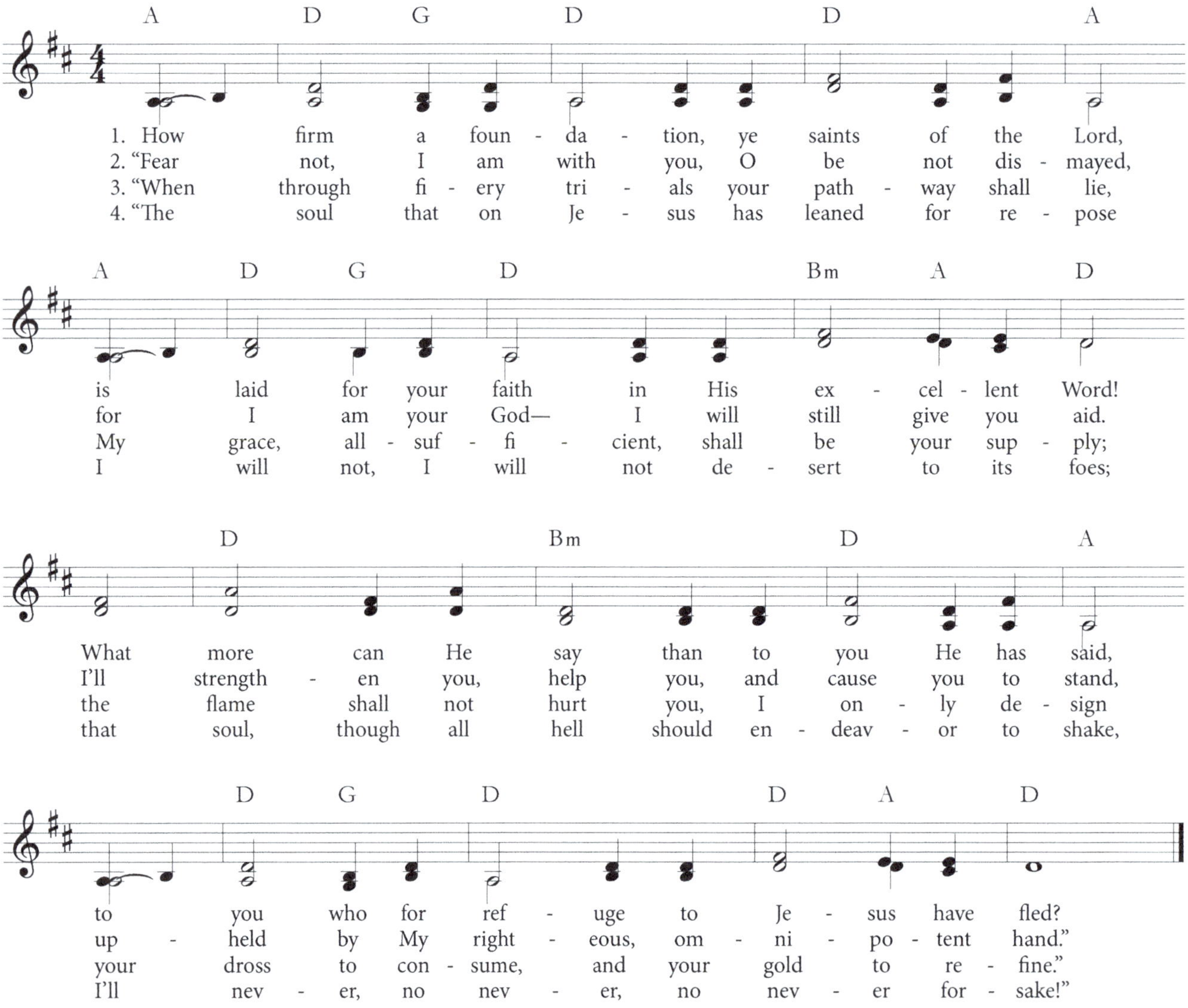

TEXT: "K" in John Rippon's *A Selection of Hymns*, 1787, alt.
MUSIC: American folk tune, Funk's *Genuine Church Music*, 1832

FOUNDATION

Jesus, What a Friend For Sinners!

"I have not come to call the righteous, but sinners to repentance." Luke 5:32

TEXT: J. Wilbur Chapman, 1907
MUSIC: Rowland Prichard, 1830

HYFRYDOL

May the Mind of Christ, My Savior

Have this attitude in yourselves which was also in Christ Jesus... Philippians 2:5

TEXT: Kate B. Wilkinson, 1925
MUSIC: A. Cyril Barham-Gould, 1925

ST. LEONARDS
87.85

My Shepherd Will Supply My Need

Surely goodness and lovingkindness will follow me all the days of my life,
and I will dwell in the house of the Lord forever. Psalm 23:6

TEXT: Isaac Watts, 1719
MUSIC: traditional American melody

RESIGNATION

Take My Life, and Let It Be

Therefore I urge you, brethren, by the mercies of God, to present your bodies a living and holy sacrifice, acceptable to God, which is your spiritual service of worship. Romans 12:1

TEXT: Frances R. Havergal, 1874
MUSIC: Henri A. Cesar Malan, 1827

HENDON

Trust and Obey

"If you keep My commandments, you will abide in My love... These things I have spoken to you so that My joy may be in you, and that your joy may be made full." John 15:10-11

TEXT: John H. Sammis, 1887
MUSIC: Daniel B. Towner, 1887

TRUST AND OBEY

When I Survey the Wondrous Cross

He Himself bore our sins in His body on the cross, so that we might die to sin and live to righteousness; for by His wounds you were healed. 1 Peter 2:24

TEXT: Isaac Watts, 1707
MUSIC: Lowell Mason, 1824

HAMBURG

Index

Living faith shows itself by producing true works and by enduring life's trials.